What is Matter?

LIQUIDS

Cindy Rodriguez

www.av2books.com

LET'S READ

AV²
BY WEIGL™
ADDED VALUE • AUDIO VISUAL

Go to **www.av2books.com**, and enter this book's unique code.

BOOK CODE

T175689

AV² by Weigl brings you media enhanced books that support active learning.

AV² provides enriched content that supplements and complements this book. Weigl's AV² books strive to create inspired learning and engage young minds in a total learning experience.

Your AV² Media Enhanced books come alive with...

Audio
Listen to sections of the book read aloud.

Video
Watch informative video clips.

Embedded Weblinks
Gain additional information for research.

Try This!
Complete activities and hands-on experiments.

Key Words
Study vocabulary, and complete a matching word activity.

Quizzes
Test your knowledge.

Slide Show
View images and captions, and prepare a presentation.

... and much, much more!

Published by AV² by Weigl
350 5th Avenue, 59th Floor New York, NY 10118
Website: www.av2books.com   www.weigl.com

Library of Congress Cataloguing in Publication data available upon request.
Fax 1-866-449-3445 for the attention of the Publishing Records department.

ISBN 978-1-61913-603-8 (hard cover)
ISBN 978-1-61913-605-2 (soft cover)

Printed in the United States of America in North Mankato, Minnesota
1 2 3 4 5 6 7 8   16 15 14 13 12

062012
WEP170512

Editor: Aaron Carr   Design: Mandy Christiansen

Weigl acknowledges Getty Images, iStock, and Dreamstime as image suppliers for this title.

2

What is Matter?

LIQUIDS

CONTENTS

Liquids have no shape.

Liquids take up space.

4

Many things are liquids.

Liquids can pour into a container.

Liquids take the shape of their container.

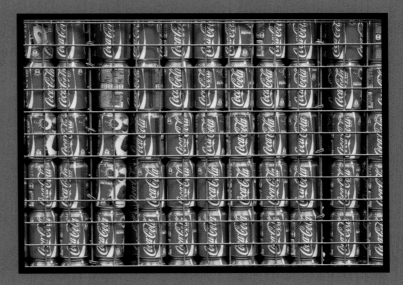

Liquids can fit
in many containers.

Liquids can be thick.

Liquids can be thin.

8

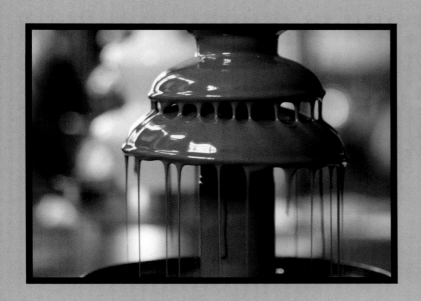

Many foods are liquids.

One liquid can feel different
from another liquid.

The way a liquid feels
is called texture.

Many liquids have texture.

 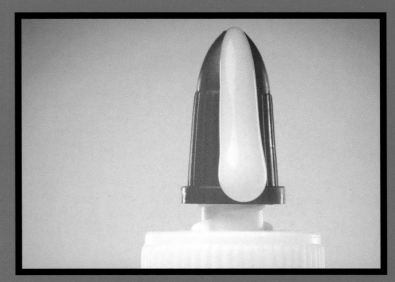

11

Liquids are one kind of matter.

Solids and gases are other kinds of matter.

There are many liquids, solids, and gases.

Liquids turn into solids when they get cold.

This is called freezing.

Water turns to snow or ice when it gets cold.

Liquids turn to gases when they get hot.

This is called boiling.

Water turns to steam when it gets hot.

The Sun can change liquids.

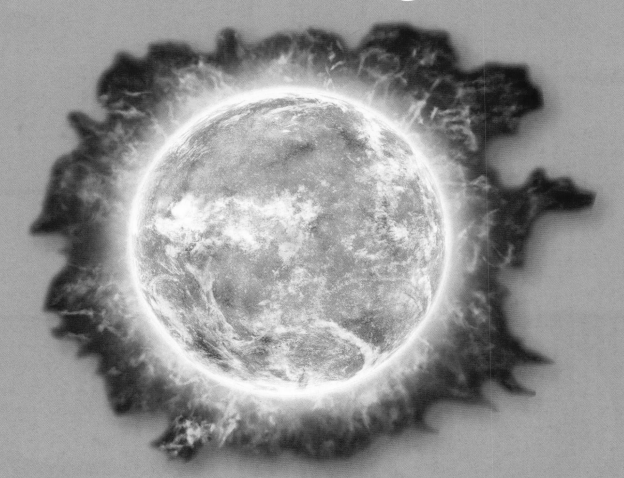

The Sun heats up water.

Heat turns water into a gas.

19

Water is an important kind of matter.

Water can be a liquid, solid, or gas.

Many things
are made of water.

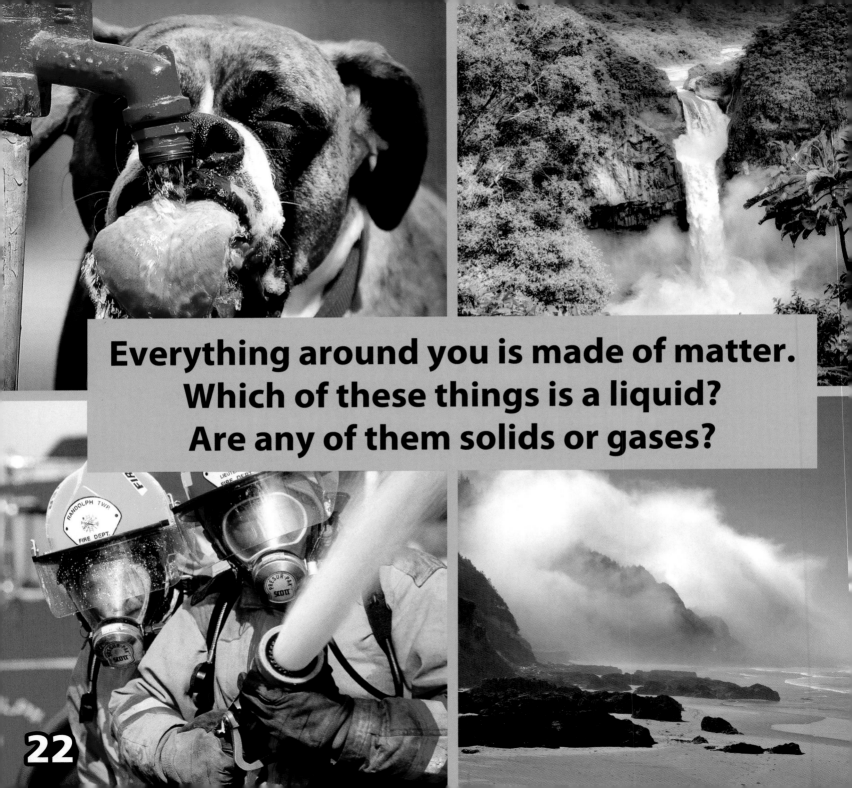

Everything around you is made of matter.
Which of these things is a liquid?
Are any of them solids or gases?

Are any of these liquids boiling or freezing?

23

KEY WORDS

Research has shown that as much as 65 percent of all written material published in English is made up of 300 words. These 300 words cannot be taught using pictures or learned by sounding them out. They must be recognized by sight. This book contains 44 common sight words to help young readers improve their reading fluency and comprehension. This book also teaches young readers several important content words. These words are paired with pictures to aid in learning and improve understanding.

Page	Sight Words First Appearance
4	are, have, many, no, take, things, up
6	a, can, in, into, of, the, their
8	be, foods
10	another, different, from, is, one, way
12	and, kind, other, there
14	get, it, or, they, this, to, water, when
18	change
20	an, important, made
22	any, around, them, these, which, you

Page	Content Words First Appearance
4	liquids, shape, space
6	container
10	texture
12	gases, matter, solids
14	ice, snow
16	boiling, steam
18	Sun

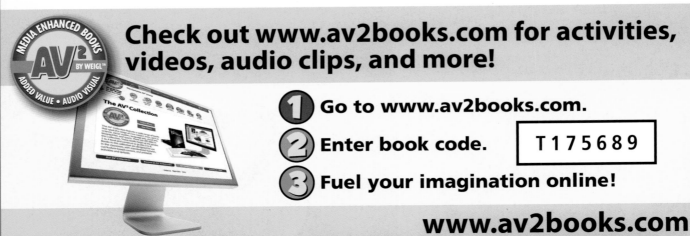

Check out www.av2books.com for activities, videos, audio clips, and more!

1 Go to www.av2books.com.

2 Enter book code. T175689

3 Fuel your imagination online!

www.av2books.com